Country Life

Wayland

Titles in the series

Cover illustrations: Background – 1517 woodcut showing country life; Inset – *The parable of the rich man who built greater barns* by Abel Grimmer, late 16th century.

First published in 1993 by Wayland (Publishers) Ltd
61 Western Road, Hove, East Sussex BN3 1JD, England

© Copyright 1993 Wayland (Publishers) Ltd

Editor: Cath Senker
Designer: John Christopher
Picture researcher: Tony D. Triggs
Consultant: Linda Goddard, Primary History Advisory Teacher,
Runnymede Staff Development Centre, Surrey

British Library Cataloguing in Publication Data
Triggs, Tony D.
  Country Life – (Tudors and Stuarts series)
  I. Title II. Series
  942

ISBN 0-7502-0762-0

Typeset by Strong Silent Type
Printed and bound by B.P.C.C. Paulton Books, Great Britain

Notes for teachers

Country Life draws on a wide range of exciting sources, including maps, artefacts, drawings and inventories. This book:

◆ compares rich and poor people's homes in the countryside and shows how country homes changed over the period;

◆ describes how villagers farmed, and looks at other kinds of work country people did, such as producing cloth from wool and milling flour;

◆ shows why the Kett rebellion occurred;

◆ looks at how some villages disappeared during Tudor and Stuart times and suggests ways of finding out about them;

◆ helps the reader to understand how to use clues from the past, such as inventories and maps, to learn about how people lived in Tudor and Stuart times.

Picture acknowledgements

Abbey House Museum, Leeds 21 (above); L & R Adkins 4 (above), 9 (both), 12, 20 (both), 22, 25 (above), 26 (above); Bodleian Library (ms Wills Peculiar 66/3/1) 7 (above), (ms Maps Notts a.2) 8 (below), (2704.d.46) 15 (below), (ms Wills Oxon 58/2/23) 23; Bridgeman *cover* (inset) and title page; G A Dey 11 (below); English Heritage 18 (both); Folger Shakespeare 26 (below); L Goodsell 16, 17; Mansell 8 (above), 27; Museum of London 21 (below); National Trust (J Bethell) 5 and 24, 25 (below); Peter Newark *cover* (background); Science Museum 13; Shakespeare Birthplace Trust 6 (both); Wayland 10 (both); David Williams Picture Library 4 (below), 7 (below); R Wood 14; York Archaeological Trust (A Crawshaw) 19 (above); Artwork: John Yates 11 (above), 15 (above), 19 (below). Ordnance Survey Pathfinder map (1986) reproduced with the permission of the Controller of Her Majesty's Stationery Office, Crown Copyright.

Contents

Wealthy Tudors at home

The Tudor kings and queens ruled England and Wales from 1485 to 1603, and the Stuarts ruled England, Scotland and Wales from 1603 to 1714. During that time most people lived in simple homes in villages.

Wealthy Tudors had very fine homes in the countryside. They showed off their wealth by making their houses as large as they could, but people today might find them cold and uncomfortable.

(Above) A fine Tudor house at Brympton d'Evercy in Somerset.

(Left) Huntingtower Castle, near Perth, Scotland. It was built when Henry VIII was ruling in England and James V was ruling in Scotland.

4

Visiting Tudor homes

We can still visit large Tudor homes today. We need to try to imagine them without modern heating and electric lights. For warmth, the servants burnt wood or coal in huge fireplaces, but the houses stayed chilly just the same. The cold stone walls seemed to take away much of the heat.

The photograph below shows how wealthy Tudors sometimes hung tapestries on their walls to keep out the cold. It also shows the curtains they hung round their beds to keep themselves warm at night.

The main bedroom at Hardwick Hall in Derbyshire.

Poor people's homes

Most people lived in villages, in simple homes built of stone or wood. If you look at the farmhouse on the right you can see the wooden beams clearly. The gaps between them were filled with twigs, which were covered with plaster.

(Right) This farmhouse near Stratford-upon-Avon is called Anne Hathaway's Cottage.

Most of these homes have been pulled down and the ones that still exist often have today's furnishings inside them.

Simple possessions

If we want to know what furniture people used to have, we can study the lists that were sometimes made.

(Left) The kitchen in Anne Hathaway's Cottage.

In 1550 a man called Thomas Coner, who lived near Oxford, died. His friends made a list of all his possessions (the things he owned), so they could share them out according to Coner's will.

10 fields of wheat	2 coverlets and 2 blankets
12 fields of barley	3 towels and 4 meat cloths
7 fields of beans	12 plates and 12 saucers
4 horses	4 candlesticks
6 cows	4 pots and two pans
7 pigs and 8 piglets	1 cart with metal-rimmed
1 feather bed and	wheels
a bed stuffed with wool	1 brooch
7 pairs of sheets	A plough with all its fittings.

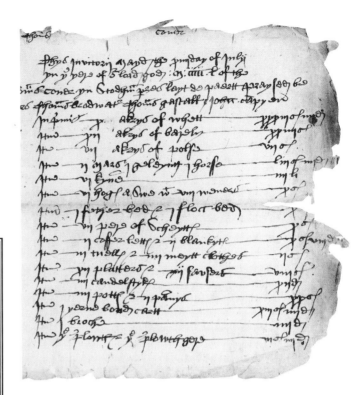

(Above) The list of Coner's possessions in his friends' writing.
(Left) The list in modern English.

You can easily work out what Thomas Coner had done for a living. You can also pick out other clues about his life. For example, you can tell how he lit his home in the long, dark winter evenings. Remember that the list tells us everything Coner owned when he died. Would you say that he was rich or poor?

Building with stone

Builders used stone to build the houses in Culross, even though they were only for poor people. The houses have lasted to the present day, although some things, like the roofs, have been changed.

A late sixteenth-century house, Culross, Scotland.

Village life

Many villages had fields which were divided up into strips. Each family farmed some separate strips in every field, so everyone had some of the good soil and some of the poor, stony soil.

We know about this way of farming from very old maps like the one belows. Study the map and try to pick out the fields and the strips.

(Above) Villagers making hay in the early seventeeth century.

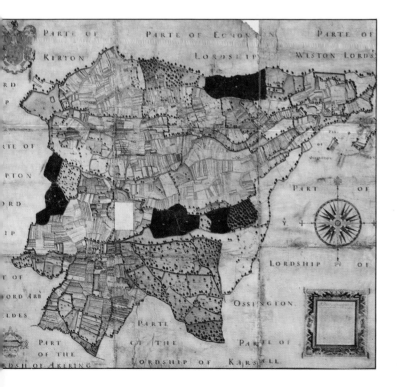

Many villages had three main fields. Usually, one field had beans, another had sheep and the third had a crop like wheat or barley. The villagers kept the sheep in a different field each year, so every field got a share of their dung, and this kept the soil rich.

(Left) This map of Laxton in Nottinghamshire was drawn in 1635.

The two most important people in a village were the priest and the landlord. The landlord owned most of the land and the houses. The villagers had to pay him rent, and some of them had to work on his land for a few days a year.

Although most villagers were very poor, some of them managed to buy their homes and the land they farmed.

This large sixteenth-century tithe barn in Dunster, Somerset, still stands today.

A share for the priest

The villagers had to give the priest a share of their crops. The priest's usual share was a tithe, or tenth, and the villagers took it to a barn called a tithe barn.

An archaeologist digging up the remains of a tithe barn.

Work for all the family

In spring, country people sheared their sheep. They used the wool to make clothes for themselves, and they sold their extra cloth to merchants.

Turning wool into cloth

Women and girls did most of the work of making cloth. First, they used special combs to get rid of the tangled bits in the wool. Once the wool was straightened out they spun it into woollen thread. Then they wove it into cloth on a frame called a loom.

(Above) Rats ruined crops and stocks of food. This man (and his cat) earned his living by killing them.

(Left) A mid-seventeenth century picture of a woman using a spinning-wheel to spin wool into thread.

You can weave your own cloth on a simple loom like the one on the right. Tie some woollen threads to the top and bottom of your loom. Then take some more wool and weave it over and under the threads. Go from side to side across your loom to make a piece of cloth.

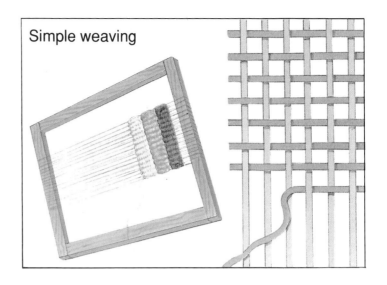

Simple weaving

Harvest time

In autumn, villagers gathered all their crops from the fields. They sometimes gathered their newly-cut wheat, barley or oats into clumps called stooks. Later they took it away and threshed (beat) it to get the seeds, called grain.

People today sometimes use old methods when they do not have machinery. The man in the photo is making a stook from bunches of oats tied together with straw. Making stooks by hand needs a lot of skill. He probably learned how to do it from older people when he was a child.

We cannot be sure how Tudor and Stuart farmers made stooks, but skills like this are often passed on for centuries.

After the grain had been removed, the straw was used for thatching roofs. Thatching is another skill that has been passed on for hundreds of years.

A modern farmer gathering oats into stooks.

After the harvest

This carving in a Somerset church shows a mill and a miller. Was the mill driven by wind or water? How did the miller carry his flour?

Today we can store food in tins or freezers to keep it good. Tudor and Stuart people had to find other ways to store food. They added salt to meat to stop it from going bad, and they dried other food like peas and beans.

Grinding the grain

Millers were very important in Tudor and Stuart times. They ground the villagers' grain into flour for making bread (and they kept a share of the flour for themselves).

Some mills were built beside streams. The water turned a wheel and the wheel turned a huge, flat stone inside the mill, which ground the grain.

Other mills were built on hills. They had huge sails to catch the wind, and the wind did the work of turning the stone.

Mills outside a town in the late sixteenth century.

Learning from pictures

We have to look at pictures very carefully because artists do not always show things just as they are in real life. In the picture above, the artist has shown lots of mills near a town, but in fact the mills were scattered around the countryside. Why do you think he put all the mills together in one picture?

There are lots of things you can learn from this picture. You can see the round stones that were used in a mill. You can also see part of a poor person's house and compare it with buildings in the town. Try to find two or three different ways of carrying goods, and try to pick out a damaged mill that was no longer being used.

Change and rebellion

Tudor landlords found that they could earn a lot of money by selling wool or woollen cloth. They started keeping extra sheep on land that villagers had always shared. The villagers were suddenly short of land and they found it hard to feed themselves and their own sheep and cattle.

Robert Kett's rebellion

Landlords did not need many workers to care for their sheep. Some of them put up rents to make the villagers leave, and thousands had to go begging in towns. Country people were angry at the way they were being treated. Some demanded new laws to stop landlords from taking so much land.

In 1549 a man called Robert Kett led a rebellion in Suffolk and Norfolk. He and thousands of followers set up a camp outside Norwich. They took over the city, but soldiers came and attacked their camp. They seized Robert Kett, locked him up and put him to death.

On the right is a map showing what happened during Kett's rebellion.

This tree is known as Kett's Oak. It is said that Kett and his followers met at the tree before going to Norwich with their complaints.

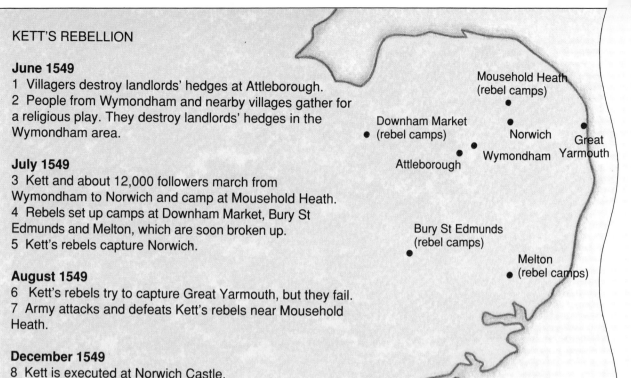

KETT'S REBELLION

June 1549
1 Villagers destroy landlords' hedges at Attleborough.
2 People from Wymondham and nearby villages gather for a religious play. They destroy landlords' hedges in the Wymondham area.

July 1549
3 Kett and about 12,000 followers march from Wymondham to Norwich and camp at Mousehold Heath.
4 Rebels set up camps at Downham Market, Bury St Edmunds and Melton, which are soon broken up.
5 Kett's rebels capture Norwich.

August 1549
6 Kett's rebels try to capture Great Yarmouth, but they fail.
7 Army attacks and defeats Kett's rebels near Mousehold Heath.

December 1549
8 Kett is executed at Norwich Castle.

Map labels: Mousehold Heath (rebel camps), Downham Market (rebel camps), Norwich, Great Yarmouth, Attleborough, Wymondham, Bury St Edmunds (rebel camps), Melton (rebel camps)

Timeline

About 1500

Tudor landowners start to enclose common land for their sheep.

1549

Kett's rebellion.

1552

A famous leaflet blames sheep farmers for causing poverty.

Complaints in the Midlands

In a leaflet of 1552, people from the Midlands complained that landlords were charging too much for their wool and mutton (meat from sheep):

> "*The more sheep, the dearer is the wool.*
> *The more sheep, the dearer is the mutton.*"

They also complained at the way other prices were rising:

> "*The more sheep, the dearer is the beef.*
> *The more sheep, the dearer is the corn...*
> *The more sheep, the fewer eggs for a penny.*"

The extra sheep were being blamed for everything!

(Below) Part of the leaflet which appeared in 1552.

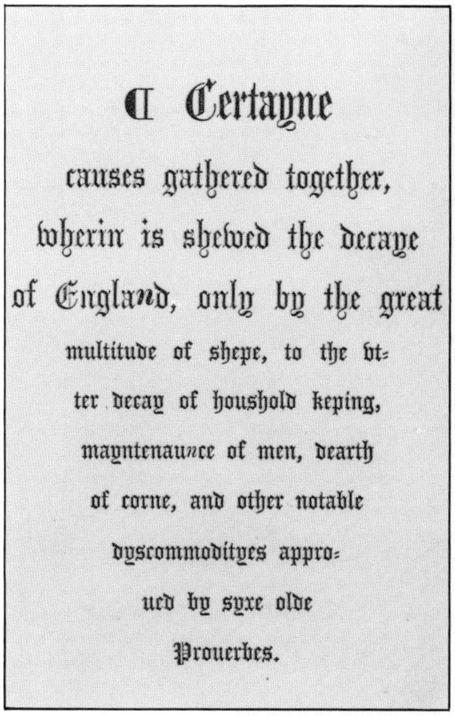

> ❡ Certayne
> causes gathered together,
> wherin is shewed the decaye
> of England, only by the great
> multitude of shepe, to the vt-
> ter decay of houshold keping,
> mayntenaunce of men, dearth
> of corne, and other notable
> dyscommodityes appro-
> ued by syxe olde
> Prouerbes.

Lost villages

In some parts of England the rich took so much land for sheep that nearly everyone had to leave. A disease called the plague also cut down the number of people in many villages.

Some villages were left with no people at all, and the houses fell into ruins and slowly disappeared. We can often tell where these villages, called 'lost' villages, stood.

Finding lost villages

Modern maps can give us clues to help us to find lost villages. Some of the clues on this map have been marked, but perhaps you can pick out some more for yourself.

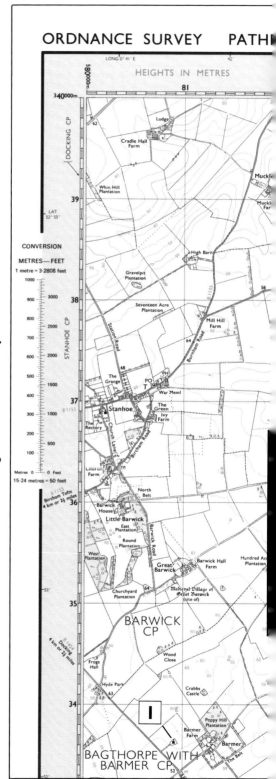

KEY

1 This sign means 'church'. The dotted line shows a footpath leading to empty fields. Perhaps there was once a village there.

2 Ruined churches in empty fields nearly always show where lost villages stood.

3 The cross marks a little church. But what is left of the village now?

4 Sometimes little more than a place name is left.

5 Sometimes, as well as a ruined church, we can see a pattern of humps that shows where houses stood.

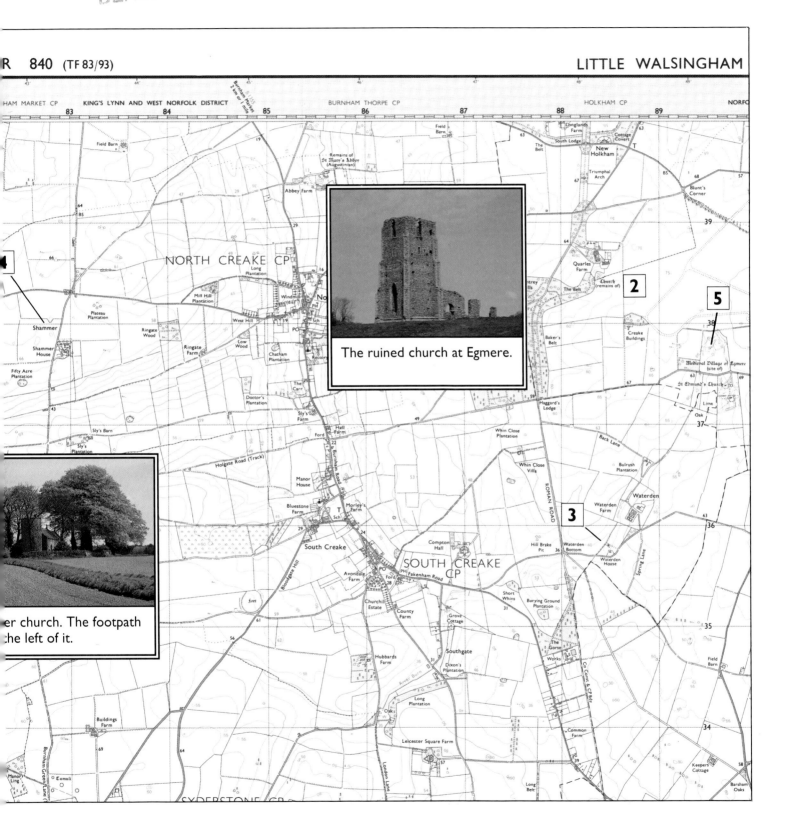

R 840 (TF 83/93)   LITTLE WALSINGHAM

The ruined church at Egmere.

...er church. The footpath
...he left of it.

Finding out more about lost villages

Archaeologists study the past from remains, and sometimes they find the remains of a lost village. They can dig them up and find out how the people there used to live.

(Below) **The remains of Wharram Percy, a lost village in Yorkshire. It slowly disappeared in Tudor and Stuart times. You can see the ruins of the church in front of a modern farmhouse.**

(Above) **A modern drawing showing how Wharram Percy looked before it disappeared.**

Pictures from aircraft

When old garden walls and the walls of old buildings fall down, they sometimes leave bumps and dips in a field. Pictures taken from aircraft often show them clearly, especially when there is snow on the ground.

(Right) A picture of Wharram Percy from the air.

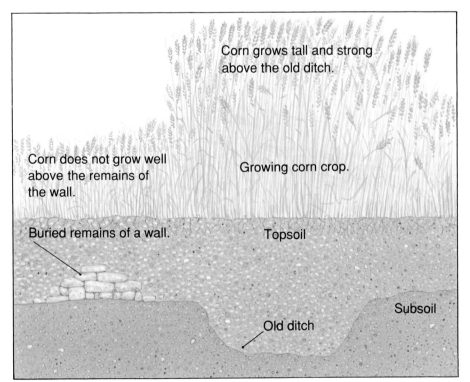

Corn grows tall and strong above the old ditch.

Corn does not grow well above the remains of the wall.

Growing corn crop.

Buried remains of a wall.

Topsoil

Old ditch

Subsoil

This drawing shows how buried walls and ditches affect crops.

Clues that grow!

Buried walls and ditches can affect growing crops, even when the surface of the ground is smooth. Stones from old walls make the plants small and weedy; old ditches help them to grow tall and strong. A smooth patch of ground can grow a very uneven crop, so archaeologists study fields in the summer sun as well as in the snow.

Difficult journeys

Villagers sometimes took food to towns and sold it in markets. Travelling from place to place was very difficult, especially in Tudor times. Villagers and merchants often had to ride through mud and water. They were glad when they found small bridges like the one on the right.

(Above) This bridge at Dunster, Somerset, was used in Tudor and Stuart times.

Improvements to roads

In Tudor times, the people of every village had to look after local roads themselves. A gang of villagers had to do a few days' repair work every year.

The system did not work very well. Villages were sometimes short of men, or there was no local stone for filling holes. Many roads were very bad, and travellers sometimes got stuck in mud.

(Left) Merchants went on long and difficult journeys abroad in ships like the one in this carving.

The Stuart Parliament tried to solve these problems. In 1663 it told some county councils to repair an important road north of London. This was better than leaving the job to the people in the villages through which it ran. The repairs cost a lot of money, so the councils made travellers pay a charge called a toll when they used the road.

TABLE of WEIGHTS

Towed in Winter and Summer to Carriages directed to be weighed (including the Carriage and Loading) by the Act of the 4th, George the 4th.

	Summer 1st May to 31st October Both Inclusive		Winter 1st November to 30th April Both Inclusive	
	Tons	Cwts	Tons	Cwts
For every Waggon with nine inch Wheels	6	10	6	0
For every Cart with nine inch Wheels	3	10	3	0
For every Waggon with six inch Wheels	4	15	4	5
For every Cart with six inch Wheels --	3	0	2	15
For every Waggon with Wheels of the breadth of four inches and a half - -	4	5	3	15
For every Cart with Wheels of the breadth of four inches and a half - -	2	12	2	7
For every Waggon with Wheels of less than four inches and a half - - - - -	3	15	3	5
For every Cart with Wheels of less than four inches and a half - - - -	1	15	1	10

TABLE of TOLLS for OVERWEIGHT

directed to be taken by 3rd, George 4th, cap, 126. sec. 15.

	For	
	s	d
For the first and second Hundred weight (of 112lb to the Hundred) of Overweight which any Wag		

(Above) An eighteenth-century list of waggon weights, upon which tolls were based.

Soon there were similar roads throughout Britain, and stage-coach companies began to use them for regular journeys between the main towns. We know about stage-coach services from posters and advertisements.

The service from York to London took four days, so passengers had to spend three nights at inns. Nowadays, the journey takes two hours by train.

PIAZZA in Coventgarden,

A drawing from about 1640. You can see a stage-coach on the left.

Villages that grew into towns

Many villages disappeared in the sixteenth and seventeenth centuries, but others grew into busy towns. Some villages grew because stage-coaches called there. Traders moved in to sell goods to the travellers.

The horses that pulled the coaches had to be changed for fresh ones every two or three hours. Inns were built by roads, and the inn-keepers kept a supply of fresh horses. They also had beer, food and beds for tired travellers!

Wealthy traders

Some villages in south-east England, Shropshire, Herefordshire and Wales became centres for the trade in wool and cloth. These villages grew into small country towns, and we can still see the merchants' magnificent houses.

Many wealthy merchants lived in this street in Ledbury, Herefordshire.

Better off in town?

In 1590 a woman called Elinor Simkins died in Chipping
Norton in Oxfordshire. Chipping Norton was growing into
a busy market town. Look back at page 7 and compare
Elinor Simkins's possessions with those of William Coner.

Part of the list of Elinor Simkins's possessions.

In the parlour	a stone bowl	a big brass pan
a table	a saucepan	3 kettles
a bench	3 small brass pots	a brass pot
a stool	2 small kettles	a sieve
a chest	a wheel for spinning	a tub
a shelf	wool	a stand for supporting
4 wooden dishes	2 clay pots	pots over a fire
a set of 12 wooden	a sieve	a frying pan
plates	a pair of bellows	a beer barrel
a skimmer [for		an iron bar
skimming the cream		a little container for
off milk]	**In the kitchen**	milk or butter
22 other wooden	a table	a washing tub
plates	a tool for grinding	2 pails
2 saucers	barley	a ladle
7 spoons	a huge cooking pot	some odds and ends

The list in modern English.

From 1600

Wharram Percy in Yorkshire loses its people.

1663

Councils and companies start to look after many roads.

From the 1660s

Farmers begin to grow crops found in the Americas, such as potatoes and maize.

1690s

New stage-coach services link big towns. Some villages on the route slowly grow into busy towns.

Country homes for the rich

We can still look round the fine country homes that
were built in Tudor and Stuart times. Often, we can see
that the Stuarts spent even more money on beautiful
decorations than people had done in Tudor times.

**A room at Ham House,
Surrey. It still looks much
the same as it did in 1635.**

This magnificent building, called a gatehouse, was just for a servant.
Think what the owner's house must have been like!

Beautiful rooms

Glass was still expensive in Stuart times, just as it had been in Tudor times, so houses often had rather small windows. Some wealthy Stuarts used coloured window panes and arranged them in patterns to make 'rose windows'.

They tried to make their rooms seem bright by using white plaster and gleaming gold paint on the walls and ceilings. The plaster and gold paint reflected the light of the lamps and candles.

Tapestries were still used to keep out the cold. The tapestries, paintings and decorations often came from foreign countries.

The 'rose window' at East Riddlesden Hall in West Yorkshire.

25

Pleasures and pastimes

People in Tudor and Stuart times enjoyed themselves in different ways, depending on how much money they had. The poor had to make do with things that cost nothing; the rich had very expensive pleasures.

A drawing of a maze of hedges in a sixteenth-century garden.

Rich people's pleasures

Rich Tudor and Stuart people liked fancy things. They had enormous gardens, and they made their gardeners grow hedges in a complicated pattern to make a maze. In summer they let their guests explore the maze. They probably laughed when the guests lost their way and bumped into each other.

(Above) Rich people liked to go riding and hunting. This building at Kenilworth, Warwickshire, used to be stables.

Poor people's games

Poor people sometimes stuffed a pig's bladder and used it to play a rough sort of football. There was no proper pitch. Each team tried to get the ball to a different place in the village.

According to a writer called Sir Thomas Elyot:

" *Sometimes their necks are broken, sometimes their backs, sometimes their arms... It is nothing but beastly fury and extreme violence.* "

Sir Thomas probably enjoyed gentler pastimes!

(Left) These people have made a see-saw from a plank and a barrel. Do you think they are wealthy or poor?

Timeline

1480	1500	1520	1540	1560	1580

Tudors

1485 HENRY VII

1509 HENRY VIII

1547 EDWARD VI

1553 MARY TUDOR

1558 ELIZABETH I

1480–1500	1500–1520	1520–1540	1540–1560	1560–1580	1580–1600
1492 Columbus sails to America.	**1500–1547** Sheep farmers enclose common land.	**1520** The Spaniards begin to settle on the American mainland.	**1543** The Belgian-born scientist Andreas Vesalius publishes his book about the human body.	**1567** As a Catholic, Mary Queen of Scots flees from Scotland but is imprisoned in England.	**1587** Mary Queen of Scots is executed.
	1509 Cabot tries to sail round the north of Canada.	**1534** Henry VIII becomes Head of the Church in England and Wales.	**1547–1553** Many schools and colleges are built.	**1577** Sir Francis Drake sets off on his voyage around the world.	**1588** The Spanish Armada is defeated.
	1500 – 1600 Rents rise and many poor villagers move to the towns to look for work.	**1536** Henry VIII's second wife, Anne Boleyn, is put to death.	**1549** Robert Kett leads a rebellion in Norfolk.		**1595** Sir Walter Raleigh explores South America.
		1539 Henry VIII has the monasteries destroyed.	**1550 – 1650** Newcastle grows because of the coal and lead mines.		**1590–1616** William Shakespeare writes his plays.
			1553–1558 Protestants are persecuted and put to death.		

1600	**1620**	**1640**	**1660**	**1680**	**1700**

Stuarts

1603 JAMES I (JAMES VI OF SCOTLAND)

1625 CHARLES I

1649–1660 COMMONWEALTH
1653 OLIVER CROMWELL
1658 RICHARD CROMWELL
1660 CHARLES II

1685 JAMES II
1688 WILLIAM III & MARY II

1702–1714 ANNE

1600–1620	1620–1640	1640–1660	1660–1680	1680–1700	1700–1710

1600–1620

1605
The Gunpowder Plot.

1607
The explorer Henry Hudson sets off to the coast of northern Canada.

1610
Hudson discovers a huge bay in northern Canada. He names it Hudson Bay.

1620
The Puritan Pilgrim Fathers sail from England to settle in America.

1620–1640

1628
The scientist William Harvey describes how blood goes round the body.

1630–1641
Charles I rules without Parliament.

1640–1660

1642
The Civil War begins.

1646
Charles I is captured and imprisoned.

1649
Charles I is executed.

1649–1660
England, Scotland and Wales are ruled without a king or queen.

1660
The Restoration of the monarchy. Charles II becomes king.

1660–1680

1665
The plague.

1666
The Great Fire of London.

1660–1669
Samuel Pepys writes his diary about life during the Restoration.

1660–1685
Scientists Robert Hooke and Isaac Newton study light and gravity. Sir Christopher Wren designs many buildings in London.

1660–1700
Coffee houses become popular.

1680–1700

1690
The Battle of the Boyne.

1694
Queen Mary dies.

1667–1695
The composer Henry Purcell writes his music.

1700–1710

1707
England and Scotland are officially united.

Glossary

Archaeologist A person who studies the past from remains.

Beams Long, strong pieces of wood that are used for building.

Cottage A small, simple home.

Council A group of people that runs a town or a larger part of the country.

County A large area, such as Yorkshire or Aberdeenshire.

Inn A small hotel, often used by travellers.

Landlord Someone who owns and rents out land or homes.

Loom A special frame that is used for weaving cloth.

Miller Someone who works in a mill, grinding grain into flour.

Shear To cut the wool off a sheep.

Stables Sheds where horses are kept.

Stage-coach A covered coach that was pulled by horses. Each stage-coach used to follow a particular route.

Tapestries Pieces of cloth with a woven design. Tapestries were used to cover walls.

Thatching Covering a roof with straw.

Tithe A tenth part of a crop, usually given to the Church.

Toll A fee paid for using a road.

Will A document saying what someone wants done with his or her things after death.

Books to read

Carter, M., Culpin, C. & Kinloch, N. *Past into Present 2: 1400-1700* (Collins Educational, 1990)

James, A. *Castles and Mansions* (Wayland, 1988)

Kelly, T. *Children in Tudor England* (Thornes and Hulton, 1987)

Martin, Christopher *Spotlight on the Agricultural Revolution* (Wayland, 1986) For older readers.

Triggs, T. D. *Tudor and Stuart Times* (Folens, 1992)

Triggs, T.D. *Tudor Britain* (Wayland, 1989)

Wood, T. *The Stuarts* (Ladybird, 1991)

Places to visit

Country houses

East Riddlesden Hall, W. Yorkshire

Hardwick Hall, Derbyshire

Little Moreton Hall, Cheshire

Longleat House, Wiltshire

Castles and fortifications

Berwick-on-Tweed, Northumberland

Drumlanrig Castle, Thornhill, Dumfriesshire

Kenilworth Castle, Warwickshire

Portland, Dorset

Southsea, Hampshire

Walmer Castle, near Deal in Kent

Poor people's houses

Culross, near Dunfermline, Fife, Scotland

Museum

National Museum of Wales, Welsh Folk Museum, St Fagans, Cardiff

Index

Words printed in **bold** are subjects that are shown in pictures as well as in the text.